AF620023

Into the Eye

by Scott Hill

Into the Eye

ISBN: 978-1-71666-638-4

Into the Eye Poems

Status Quo I

Lights flicker from my room
As heavy winds foreshadow doom
    I stand with broken mirrors in a smiling costume
I knew I was insane
As metal bullets caused disdain
    From bouncing through my head and leaving me with bloodstains
Clenching both my fists
From writing useless lists
    Of good intentions ruined and tattooed upon my wrists
The walls begin to whirl
And the ceiling forms a swirl
    The tunnels of my vision cause my thoughts to bend and twirl
So I quickly grab the meds
And I think of all my dreads
    Of snakes and spiders crawling in and out and through my head
My stormy path is shown
And the help I had postponed
    Is thrashing all around me like a twisted cyclone

Maybe This Time

Morning.

I frantically opened my eyes
To close my jar of scares
And was gently greeted by January's silver laughter

"Come eat with us"

I rolled over to find debris and strangers in my tent
Wiped my brow and sat up in the ashes, shivering

I recalled the midnight before

Yes, it was midnight when I realized how similar
Life could be to opening a bottle of champagne

It was a battle to pop the top on cue
And timing is everything
I had missed the mark
I always do

"Come eat with us"

Did someone whisper to me? A hiss? The wind?
We were camping so perhaps it was
The chuckling of cicadas through their teeth

But then I blinked and suddenly it was night again

The whispers continued from the fire
And all my ears could gather was
Gossip of red grudges and wilting yellow lows

"Come drink with us"

Am I thirsty?
When I looked up, there were the strangers
Sipping marvelous mimosas and
Singing in an unfamiliar unison

But I was numb to their fun, I was blood-cold

These people had golden goals,
Violet passions, innocent blue hopes
While the voices in my head granted me
Burning insecurities, foggy failures, and
Charcoal mistakes

And my brain sobbed for
My life—wasted away by dancing in circles around
And around
And around a broken clock
With my mind going nowhere as it
Holds tight to twelve for safety

I blink again and it's morning

I desperately pray to be like the others
But it's hard when you're 24
And there's only 24 hours in a day to find yourself
And there's 24 hisses in your head
Of what could go
Wrong
And you feel like the new year is already halfway
Over—

"Come play with us"

Perhaps only time will tell

Alone in the Bathroom

Night.

My brain is a leaking faucet

drip, drip

There goes all reason and rationality
As my sanity circles the drain

I'm fixated on how broken I look
My reflection resembles my parents
But I'm gazing into the eyes of someone I don't
Recognize

I can't remember the last time
I used the word "family" in conversation
Because "family" is an unfamiliar language
That I haven't yet learned to speak—

drip

I brush my teeth and wash my weary face
I still look nothing like your "brother"
I look nothing like the parents who took me in
Even though I desperately wish I could—

drip, drip

Even though I wish it didn't burn my skin to be called "son"
Even though I wish I could recognize the
Sweet sounds of nostalgia that fill the ears of others
Even though I wish I could wash the doubts
I've crafted in my hands in this sink
Even though I wish you could take the creaking house of my heart—

drip, drip

—And make it a home

drip

Insight

When I was almost nine years old, I became a man
Not because I had done anything manly
But simply because I was told I was one

I was told that there were "bad men"
"Bad men" who had killed many people
In New York on September 11, 2001
In two tall buildings

So now the "good men"
(My dad being one of them)
Were now going to get the "bad men"

So it made sense at my age
That since there were no "good men"
Left on our soil
All "good boys" were promoted to "good men"

But I'm 24 now
And I see a problem with this concept

A problem that involves no "good men" in proximity
To teach "good boys"
How to be "good men"
So the "good boys" are left
Only with pictures of their fathers

Fathers with unsmiling military faces
And burning patriotism in their eyes

And the "good boys" soon realize
That being a "good man"
Requires being a "good husband" to mothers
And being a "good father" to siblings

And since there is no training like
The way a "good man" becomes a "good soldier,"
The "good boy" is
Lost among a sea of
Fatherless "bad boys" who are just as lost
As the innocence that comes with being a boy
Before becoming
A man

So when I was told that I was "man of the house,"
You can imagine how difficult this might have been
Because I hadn't been taught how to be
A "good boy"
As the terms "sissy" and "wuss" became synonymous with "soft"
And the house I "manned"
Didn't feel like a home to me
Because I was a stranger to everyone and myself

And being a man meant growing up too quickly
And investing in stoicism
And avoiding the luxury of vulnerability
As this privilege was reserved for
"Good girls" to become
Nurturing "good women"

"Men never know what they want"

Well, how can we when as boys
We were never given this type of knowledge?
The same way Adam never learned how to be a
"Good boy"
Before biting from Eden's apple
And swallowing the sin of pride
To be passed down to generations
And generations
And generations
And generations

To me

And so we are impulsive
And so we are vengeful
And so we are cruel

And society is a bystander to an issue
That sits complacently in men like me

Generation after
Generation after
Generation

Who Are You, *Really*?

Such a tough question to answer in your twenties because as men
We don't exist without purpose or meaning in our lives
And I'm still searching for mine
But if I were to make a self-portrait of myself
This is what I would see in the mirror
Through chasms of chaos and confusion and catastrophe:

Brown eyes, dark messy hair
A simple round nose, and a
Mouth with a fat lower
Lip to match on olive skin

Mother's sad-laughing eyes
Father's small ears all above teeth
That sometimes spill his humor
Over a face dotted with

Two

Moles

I eat, I breathe
I move, much like any
Other person that exists
But I'm different, I guess
Because I laugh like no one
I know I pray like no one
I find comfort in rainy days and
I drink coffee like an alcoholic and
I seek beauty in life's bouquet of pain
But I know if you look closely
Somewhere on this face
You can catch a glimpse
Of a cheeky smirk with
A very strange idea and
Something interesting
To say to you...

You Took Me Ziplining in New Zealand

You took me ziplining in New Zealand
Because you thought it would lift my spirits

But upon reaching the end of the ride
My heart sank with the Waiheke sun

You took me canyoning to see waterfalls
Because you thought they would cleanse me

But upon reaching the rocky shores
The sandflies assaulted my flesh

You took me trekking in Glenorchy
Because you thought it would settle me

But upon being paired with a chestnut filly
She became my worst auburn nightmare

You took me sightseeing in green pastures
Because you were desperate to show you care

And upon witnessing so much life
I forced a smile because   you did

Bicolor Disorder

We crashed into each other
Reckless and violent in nature
So our conversations are crimson
And our love is mauve and mad

We live bright like rubies
And angry like wild flames
We leave behind scarlet scars

We're bitter like cold plums
And dream in scented lavender
And we stain like rich wine

We come in two shades
Rosy and violet
Like bloody bruises
Painful and lasting

Divorce

Failure is as complicated as a funeral without a body
And the lessons learned intertwine
Like the red roses you used to buy her
And the thorns she left with your belongings

When I asked you who lost more
You told me that "everyone loses"

Having questions without answers
Comes with having resolutions without solutions
And that's how suffering is found

Your perception was that she was unhappy
Her perspective was that you owed her freedom

And you can't give coffee to a drunk
Can't buy single lost puzzle pieces
Without buying the entire puzzle again
For someone blind to the image on the box

My point of view is that
Divorce means Dying Alone and is worse than Death
Because there's Finality with Death
And there's Infinity with Marriage and its Consequences

For the corpse doesn't stay in the ground
The pain rears up when least expected
And acceptance is not a cut-and-dry process

So I run from Marriage without looking back
The way Forever and Always ran from each other
For the both of you

Pioneer

Alone you travelled west
To mend your broken heart
She cracked it in the center
And picked each piece apart

You stayed at small hotels
And tried to glue debris
You stitched it on your shoulders
A carving on a tree

But soon a storm developed
And shook you of your leaves
You found yourself with nothing
You turned to your beliefs

You begged the Lord for mercy
And asked for blessed wisdom
You found Him in your dreams
He gave you a new vision

"Rebuild yourself from scratch!"
He bellowed in command
Then gave you tools to start with
To build on your new land

Keep Off the Grass

I wasn't ready to start over
I wasn't ready to see someone else
Turn fallen ashes into rising sprouts

I wasn't ready to see you
Place a ring around someone so rosy
And expect me to shove posies of pride
Deep, deep into my pockets

I wanted the chance to warn her
I wanted her to know how grassy and green
How lush and alive our knoll once was

Does she know when to water the seeds?
Does she know how to talk to flowers?
Does she know how much sunlight is needed,
How much tender love it takes for nurturing a plant nursery?

Does she sing with the birds
And chase away your unwelcomed weeds?
Is she willing to ward off your wily predators
Who wish to consume the flesh of your happiness?

Most importantly
Will she be prepared to protect us
From Mother Nature's cold fronts and icy storms?

It's too soon to tell

So it's better that she stays away
Rather than mow over what's left of us

Because it's too soon to tell

Isolation and What I Found There

The trouble with reacting in a fight or flight response
Is that you end up bludgeoning yourself when you bolt
Or a part of you dashes when you duel
So the lines blur in behavior like a muddy mosaic

Let me backtrack

This morning, my boisterous brain warned me to save myself
And selfishly, I did, but I felt guilty and blamed my legs
For they had a mind of their own
And the one in my head could care less

I pitied myself, as I always do
And on walks like this, I searched for a sanctuary
Some form of temporary relief that I felt Nature could nurture

I went deeper into the trees, past clutters of pines
Past vines, past ivy, past leaves that were once lively
Past rhythmical insects and chattering creatures

Until my feet begged my legs for mercy
And I found myself in marshy solitude
At a shrine where I could worship my woes

But I realized I wasn't truly alone
For in the bog was a lifeless body
And it frightened me half to death

The corpse was a young man around my age in stature
With hopes wriggling through his eye sockets
And dreams dried up on his finger bones

I couldn't tell how he perished
But I could feel it in my ribs that he died alone
And realizing I had no further business here
I turned around and found my way home

Stop Saving Me

I cut my losses the way you cut your wrists
Full of pain
And full of guilt

I know that every time I'm drowning
You punish yourself for throwing a lifesaver
Close enough for me to reach
But far enough for me to give up

And that for every door I slam in your face
A car knocks you and your antlers
Into a bloody heap with just enough strength
To pick yourself back up because you're stubborn

Because I'm stubborn

Because admitting I'm wrong means that
I have more reason to doubt myself
The way a cat climbs a tree
Even when it's absolutely certain
It can't climb back down on its own

Like I said, I'm stubborn
Even when everything's my fault

And even now when you're hurt
I'm throwing band-aids at you
And screaming that your self-harm has scarred me
When really I'm angry at myself

Because my heart is not for you to wear under your sleeves
And my pain is not yours to bear on your body

God, Save Me Already

Sanity is a fickle fiend
With eight legs and beady eyes
Carefully crafting a red collage
Leaving it hanging dry

Rarely does the bastard bring
Me rest with kind relief
Instead he waits with grinding teeth
And gnaws my nights with grief

Mostly crawling through my hair
He bites my scalp and drinks
He hopes to sip upon my dreams
And change the way I think

Surely he will someday leave
I pray this all the time
Instead he builds a rotten web
And drinks all my red wine

Good Night, Loon

At night I hug my sorrow
A newborn in my arms
It's mindless like a scarecrow
But squawks in loud alarms

I water it with weeping
And feed it pitied lies
It grows—a weed in feeding
It welcomes putrid flies

A whispering big black widow
I fear for my own life
I keep under my pillow
A towel-covered knife

I bleed all on my blankets
My hair is falling out
I'm wounded and I'm anxious
I wish to drown my doubt

But there I stay on guard
My spirits feeling sore
And when my mattress gets too hard
I drift down to the floor

Foreshadowing

Once in a delusional dream
I knew something was wrong when I found
Butterflies inside the old Baytown library tapping on the
Windows like gentle raindrops
And after a step forward, I found myself in a large puddle
Where lily pads and lotus flowers floated by
Like paper boats down a dark stream

"How strange," I thought, "What does this all mean?"

An orange cat suddenly appeared and beckoned me
Beckoned me with a whistle so beautiful
It reminded me of a hymn
So I followed him through the pond
Past many bookshelves
Until
To my horror
I heard a thunderous crash

The cat let out a scream and darted toward
The ruins of a fallen oak tree that toppled
Toppled into the center of the library, leaving debris in its path

Oddly enough, a white horse stood at
The branches of the tree where I spotted
What looked like
A Human
Hand

The cat vanished
The water vanished
I ran to the aid of an older woman who lay
Trapped
Wearing a white gown
Gasping for air

And suddenly she was fading and
Strong gusts now poured through the
Opening that the fallen tree made
So I begged the woman to open her eyes
And when she finally did, she decided to
Stay

But in this dream, neither of us left this strange library

Because we couldn't.

April Showers...

For an entire month, it had rained
It rained from the skies
It rained from my eyes
It just wouldn't stop
Raining

And when it rains, it pours
It poured during one day in particular
When sorrows poured all over a gray hospital bed
All over a hospital bed in Baytown
In Baytown on a dark Thursday
On a dark Thursday that wouldn't stop pouring

So I poured out my heart
Over your heart as a green line
A green line that poured over a dark screen
A dark screen poured me nearly empty
Nearly empty that I thought I'd die

But it poured until you smiled and said—

"When"

—But it went back to raining

Fading, Fading Fast

You wrecked me when you capsized our ship in just twelve minutes
By making me your keeper with keys to your life's ending

At the age of twenty-four, you asked for permission
You wanted to leave, but I wanted you here

And I know I'm selfishly clinging to hope
But I'm begging you to stick around

So I keep squeezing your hand
And I'm reading to you

And adjusting pillows but
Your oxygen's low

Annie, please

Stay

...Bring May Flowers

For a brief period of time
I thought maybe I could be happy
With you safe at home
A sparrow with a new song to whistle

I watched as your bandaged wings
Worked hard to flutter once more
And color returned to your feathers
And vitality returned to a cage that was
Empty for far too long

Next month is your birthday
And it'll be your best one yet
Because it marks another successful year
Of you soaring through stormy skies
And tapping on our windows with tiny beak
Just to sing to us

And I suddenly feel a little less lonely
Knowing there's a sparrow who whistles with me
Even when we're far apart
Even if only for a brief period of time

Denial

You said you were worried about me
Don't be
I'm the captain of a broken boat

You said you had concerns about my choices
Don't
I've gained dusty treasures from my life's trash

You said I should slow down my drinking
Don't
Alcohol quenches my depression and
Caffeine feeds my anxiety

You said you were on your way to save me
Don't
There are others who deserve saving
More than me

You said you were worried about me
And we went over this already
But maybe you should be

But don't be

Venomous Hisses

I can't fish in these waters anymore
There are twelve water moccasins
That afflict my feet so that
I can't get a sense of direction

I can't be a brave modest creature
There's a green tree python that
Lunges at my legs so that
I'm reminded of how small I am

I can't create masterpieces
There's a cobra on my arm that
Will swallow me whole so I'd
Die as one novice piece

I can't work to be strong and fit
There's a boa constrictor around my throat
It rests on my back so that
All I might carry is weakness

I can't love in this house anymore
There's a rattlesnake in my heart with
Jolting tail upon my tongue that
Clatters me defensive to compliments

I can't think for myself in these trees
There's a black mamba in my brain that
Slithers on my passions
And strikes at my esteem

So I can't dream a better future
There are serpents all around that
Tickle me with their tongues and
Whisper sweet songs of death

Panic

The breaking point's near
It's sensed the way dogs smell storms
My skull feels fractured

Everyone's watching
Their eyes burn holes in my neck
Their tears are my sweat

My lungs clutch themselves
I'm finding it hard to breathe
Like keys I've misplaced

I'm losing my mind
There are cracks in dams I've built
And they're leaking fast

There's no use fighting
The inevitable match
Between sanity

And all of those pairs of eyes
Oh, catch me someone!
I can't stand the awful sight!

Being seen as monstrous
No, I just can't be
Seen as crazy—look away!

Overthinking

What does it look like when I think too much? Well, I'll tell you. Basically, imagine someone sitting on a couch and the couch has holes in it, everywhere. And the arms of the couch have been basically chewed off by either a dog or a rat, we don't really know what did it, but that they've been chewed off. Okay, now picture in the middle of the couch a young man with messy dark hair. Now the hair on this young man is actually a light brown color, but if you look closely, this man's hair is dark because it is laced in scabbing. That's right, scabbing. He is sitting on this chewed up couch with dark hair laced with scabbing and he's shaking and sitting on his hands. Why? Well, how else do you think the scabbing got there? He gets so anxious that he scratches his head. He scratches and scratches and scratches until his scalp begins to bleed and even when his fingernails are stained red, he still scratches to get rid of an itch. An itch that, unfortunately, he will never get rid of. But yet, he scratches. Scratches because it comforts him. And when it starts to hurt his finger bones and when blood begins to ooze over onto his forehead, he stops and sits on his hands so that he doesn't kill himself. Then, his scalp heals and he does it again. It's a never-ending cycle. Does he have a condition? Well, perhaps, but he's definitely a worrier. Perhaps he's been hurt too many times. Or perhaps he's had an unpleasant experience with other human beings. Is there a way to make the scratching stop? Probably not. Because as long as there are experiences out in the world that exist to make him think, he will think. It is impossible not to think. When you stop thinking, you become ignorant. And once you become ignorant, well, you die. And when you die, well, most likely you'll be forgotten, eventually. Just a boy with daggered fingernails and a mauled scalp in the earth and.... oh, thank you. Sorry, I didn't realize that I had started scratching my own head.

Finally Snapped

I wanted to be remembered right and warm
I wanted to stop shivering from icy seclusion
I wanted acceptance the way
The ocean with waving hands welcomes
A baby turtle crawling toward where it
Best belongs at home

But I soon learned that these tiny turtles
Have a one percent survival rate
Only
One
Percent
The chosen few

So I crafted shanks of glass from sand
And I hid in my shell from the world

And when you tried to rescue
This poor tortured creature
I snapped at your fingers
With a briny hiss because
I'm not a victim that's worthy of aid
When I only need seaweed bandages to keep my wounds salted
So that I may stay on my guard

So, I'm warning you
Stay far from my grounds
Or I'll chew off your flesh
And years from now when I am ready
I'll dig me a hole in the beach
And bury all that I loved alive
With me

Deep in the

Shores of

My murky

Heart

Bonfire

Time moved through town
Like a silent blue flame
And the trees we once planted
Were now fallen matches
Lit up by lies and fueled by gasoline grudges

And while I begged for quenching grace
You watched the orange leaves crackle
And dance and fall and shrivel up
Like a spider cowering before death

And after the apologies burnt out
I floated away in gray cigarette wisps
And you got cold and walked home
With the smell of smoke
Still clinging to your coat

Cut Off

The night that it happened
I ran to the little white church
And I kneeled before it
Feeling too inky to go inside
But too ghostly to run anywhere else

And like a long-lost friend
Pain embraced me from behind
Like a soft gray sweater
And She sat with me
While I cried blue and prayed gold

From Beneath

I don't know who to blame for our death
And I drifted toward the shore for an answer
To listen to raspy whispers of mourners
Who lay white roses at our stone

"Completely deliberate"
"It's all her fault"
"Selfish, selfish woman"
"She murdered her entire family"

I wanted to believe they were right about you
But I had died flailing in what was left of the truth

Because before you drowned us in the Atlantic
Before you ran over sandcastles and screams
Before you swerved from boulevard to beach
Before dad tried to drown out the demons with reason

You had prayed to God for help
You had pleaded with your pastor for guidance
You had petitioned with your doctor for a second evaluation
You had pushed yourself to keep swimming
As mother, sister, friend, daughter, and wife

Until you let yourself float away on your front
And you let us sink far behind to our grave

Eclipse

Alone in this cave
I've made my own prison
There's nothing to save
And no one to listen

But quick the tides change
When Moon pays a visit
The darkness is strange
And light seems to pivot

It spreads on the walls
And doesn't need reason
It twirls and it falls
A cycle of seasons

I forgot what light was
So I reached for a beam
And then without cause
It left like a dream

Alone in this cave
My past is forgiven
For hope soon awakens
When purpose is given

Hurricane Season

When you aimed for my flaws
You took something from me
The way looters took treasure
From closed stores in the storm

When I was shattering on the inside
You threw rocks at my windows
And you splashed through the puddles
And stole what was mine

When my power went out
You set me on fire
And you burned me to the ground
Since you got what you needed

But know this

I will revive
And be safe in security
While your insecurities
Will leave you in ruins

A fair warning, "friend"
It's hurricane season

You Gave Me the Blues

I was sixteen
You were nineteen
I took our three-year difference and formed a parachute out of it
As I jumped head-first deep into your blue eyes

You were Versace and I was Cunanan
You promised me a sapphire love wrapped in riches
And you called me your teenage dream

But you stole my innocence
And you took the cards I made you
And our secret car rides
And you burned all of it with careless excuses

Does he know I was in his house?
Does he know we stayed up past Twilight
Talking about our future and about how
You wanted to be with me more than him?
Does he know what you did to take advantage of me?

It's funny because just two years earlier
It was you who warned me about older flames
And how one can get burned by something so captivating

Funny how blue is the hottest part of a fire
And hurts the most
And lasts the longest
And creates the saddest music

But not anymore

Red Reputation

It took me seven years
Seven years to admit that
Through the feather pillows
And your fiery red hair
And in bright darkness

You took everything from me
And threw it to the hungry hallway wolves

I thought I deserved the consequences
I thought the way Jesus died for the sins of others
Was exactly how my reputation was meant to hang and bleed
While your ghostly followers spit on my corpse
And wished me a fate worse than death

I was wrong

There's nothing to justify harassment
I was seventeen and without parents and without a home of my own
Did that make me an easy target to you?

You didn't deserve to be a rebound
I know this and I'm sorry
But I didn't deserve to be bound to shame
I didn't deserve to have grown adults you knew follow me by car
And stalk me
And threaten me
And stab me with a dagger
Shaped like a sharp lie

Don't blame me for lying to you
When I said whatever it took to get me out
Of the fox traps you set up for me
Even when you made me fall out in front of others
Before I could make the leap myself

Nobody made you gingerly kiss me
Nobody forced you to beg me for favors
That I refused to give in my truck
Like a desperate dog in heat
Itching to impress your bitch friends
Who wore cones around their necks to contain gossip in their mouths
And to avoid scratching the guilt from their throats

Eleven pages later and seven years after
I'm saying out loud to myself:
            "Me too"

I see now why you were always so obsessed with elephants
Because they're strong and loud
            And they sure as hell never ever forget

To the People Who Hurt Me

Sitting in a therapist's office

I put down my knife and picked up my pen
With shaking hand and fragile heart

I apologize to each of you
And I forgive you all

You are the reflections in my mirror
Shadows that have held me for a ransom
That no one was willing to pay

To the ones who abandoned me on life's highway,
I hope someone gives you a map
To find what it means to love the way I did

To the ones who drove mistakes through my vampire heart,
I hope they become tales you share to teach your children

To the ones who made the first cut,
I hope you can stitch up the second that I made

And to You who suffered so much
I forgive You for giving up on Yourself
I forgive You for misdiagnosing Yourself as weak when You were ill
I forgive You for being a doctor to others
When You needed to care for Yourself
And I forgive You for seeing You as a monster
When You were also the prey

Now forgive Me, please

True Shame

When I was five, the flowers spoke to me, almost like a movie
I asked my mother to take me to the theater
    Didn't you hear?
    There was a shooting at one in Aurora, she says
    Go clean your room, she says
And the flowers continued to speak to me

When I was ten, I found that eating made me happy
I asked my mother to take me to McDonald's
    Didn't you hear?
    There was a shooting at one in San Ysidro, she says
    Go make a snack for your sisters, she says
And I silently eat my feelings away, only to puke them up later

When I was fourteen, I found myself losing my temper often
I asked my mother to fly me to my grandparents for peace
    Didn't you hear?
    There was a shooting in Ft. Lauderdale's airport, she says
    Go unclog the drains, she says
And I punched the floors until my knuckles bled

When I was eighteen, I started drinking heavily to escape
I asked my mother if I could go out downtown for the first time
    Didn't you hear?
    There was a shooting in Orlando at a night club, she says
    Go help the neighbor move her furniture, she says
And I drowned myself in Crown to quiet the noise

When I was twenty-one, I wanted to study psychology
To understand what was wrong with me
I asked my mother if I could enroll in college
    Didn't you hear?
    There have been shootings
    At the University of Texas and Virginia Tech, she says
    Go buy me some cigarettes and dinner, she says
And I did as she asked
While I chewed off the skin from my fingers in fear

When I was twenty-four, I felt afraid for my safety
And for those around me
I still felt the need to ask my mother for permission
I was desperate for her approval
I wanted to enlist in the military to feel brave
        Didn't you hear?
        Soldiers always get PTSD, she says
        Just look at the murders in Ft. Hood or D.C., she says
But mother, I need help, I say
I'm feeling alone and ashamed everyday

And to my surprise, she gave me a gun

        Don't look at me like that—for protection, she says
        For that's all you need as a man, she says
        For a man cannot show he is weak, she says

Though, I know that I am.
"Though, I know that I am."

Even the Clowns Cry

I would imagine at fancy parties
When a king is asked of political matters
That he knows nothing about
He might entertain his guests
With distractions of shiny objects
And Russian bears on unicycles
And exotic dancers whose names he never cared to learn

He juggles policies constantly
To avoid dropping them and making a mess
A mess he fears he will not be able to clean himself
A mess he never rehearsed for before agreeing to take the throne

I wonder if behind his ego mask
Perhaps there's a narcissistic memory
Of a time when he was "Donny"
A time when he was told he was special
That he was daring
That he would grow up to be a god someday
To make things that were good to be great again

Were your teachers right, Donny?
Were your friends right?
Do you feel as perfect as you strive to be?
Do you ever worry about how the whole circus
Would crumble if you admitted to a sideshow mistake?
Would the confetti turn to covfefe
And the celebrations into deliberations?
Do you fire subjects before you get burned?
Are you worried that you'll burn forever?

Spoiler alert: You won't with humility

Burns turn to scars and scars turn to wisdom
And wisdom doesn't fall off the head so easily

Remember, Donny, that even rulers wrongly reign
And that when a joke falls flat, even the clowns cry
And the world will still spin on as the show continues

Ode to Women

The most inspirational pillars are women
Hands down, cups up because here's to you
Here's to changing an unfair playing field
And making your own rules in a world of men

Here's to Eve who endured more pain than Adam
Because even though he extracted one rib to make Eve
She broke all her ribs bringing not one but two men
Two men into this world through blood

Here's to women of color
Who wear smiles on cracked tear-stained faces
Refusing to say, "Yes, sir," and "Not a problem, sir"
When the fire in their bellies boils with rage
Boils with injustice and intolerance and ignorance that they are fed
Forcing themselves to wash it down with a tall glass of pride

Here's to single mothers and housewives
And teachers and waitresses and mechanics
And doctors and dentists and lawyers and politicians
Here's to the actresses who smile with grace through rough waters
Not because a man said to but because they choose to
In a sea of sharks that harass and bully
What doesn't belong to them

Here's to the women who came forward with tattoos that read,
"Me too"
Not because they were hopping on the bandwagon
Like an exclusive club
But because they knew the cost
Of laying their reputations down before America
The way their violators laid them down unwillingly to feast upon
And they ignited themselves at the stake anyways
So that little girls could live in sunshine without being burned

Here's to the women who don't just sit their daughters down to say:
"You know you need to be careful out there"
But instead sit their sons down and say:
"Don't you dare make a woman uncomfortable
because taking you out...
...Will be easier than it was to bring you into this world"

Here's to all women
Who have always held just as much power as men
But have been trapped like fireflies in mason jars of inequality

Let them walk freely
Let them reign supreme
Let their captors fall like dominos
From the game that men made in the first place
And let every predator wake up
From the loud alarm clock that boldly declares
That their time is up

For Men to Sink Their Wisdom Teeth Into

One summer evening
A wounded mutt with lame leg
Paid our crew a visit
And before we could bark, it begged the question:
"Are you a man or a mouse?"

"I'm surely a man," said one
And the mutt asked for proof
So the one replied, "Hair of the dog"
Implying that he could outdrink the whole lot of us

"I'm surely a man," said the second
And the mutt asked for proof
So the second replied, "I'm a lucky dog"
Implying that he'd slept with
More women than most

"I know I'm a man," said the third
And before the mutt asked for proof,
The third kicked him hard in the rear
Laughing and teasing how
"It's easy to find a stick to beat a dog"

As he whimpered in pain
The mutt looked at me
"Let's get you home," I announced
So I scooped him up carefully
And carried him away

For while a mouse looks for escape
In drinks, women, and violence,
The man leads his pack to learn
That meek doesn't have to mean weak
And compassion doesn't make you a bitch

The Crocodile

Beware the crooked smile
of the creature that hides
inside the Lake counting
his scales, his meals, the bones
he spits back out of backs
he chewed until his belly was full
and his pockets were satisfied

Beware, for though the Wood is big
his heart is rather small and
he cares not for visitors unless
you bring him sweets and meats
that he can sink his jaws into
for he cares not of the poor
outside if inside he is rich

Beware the coming storms
and retreat to higher ground
where sits his Sanctuary Swamp
and pray, pray the pain away
but don't expect to get too
close and watch your children
for he's wily if not watched

Houston Strong

As the days blur and I stand in deep puddles
I grieve for my great city and its losses
For the families who have lost their houses
And the homes who have lost their families

But there is something to be said about what happens after

Not all life ends the way we might imagine
Not all hope decays and dies out with the storm
Not all things good and valuable are drowned

My faith is restored when people and pets are reunited
When shelter is provided from schools and churches
When swarms of volunteers outnumber mosquitos
And more prayers are held than pride or politics

When brown mud becomes a symbol for new magnolia trees
And helpful canoes find their way on the news
And neighborhood floods sail friendships
As strangers come Harvey, hell, or high water

That is what truly makes us victors over victims
That is what makes us survivors of strength

World Series

3...2...1...

Pitch...Swing...Win...Kings...Bat...Run...Number...One...
Slide...Safe...Home...Plate...Curve...Throw...Always...Pro

See, I don't know baseball, but let me tell you WHAT
I never saw Houston jumping covered up in CUTS

When the ball goes UP, and the crowd goes NUTS
I never saw a city swim its way out of a RUT

White, orange, navy blue, crowd screaming GO 'STROS!
Seeing Carlos Correa go from hero to GOAT

We got homeruns for DAYS, Alex Bregman's a BOSS
He's got CONFIDENCE and SKILLS and he won't take the LOSS...

So Pitch...Swing...Win...Kings...Bat...Run...Number...One...
Slide...Safe...Home...Plate...Curve...Throw...Always...Pro

And Verlander keeps it Upton, while Altuve keeps it humble
George Springer's so SMOOTH, he's got TWO rings for DOUBLE

Man, we OWNED the World Series and we didn't come to play
We'll be keeping all our CROWNS in the club at MINUTE MAID...

And Pitch...Swing...Win...Kings...Bat...Run...Number...One...
Slide...Safe...Home...Plate...Curve...Throw...Always...Pro

You see, it's not about baseball, it's all about our PRIDE
It's all about seeing that the clouds have silver LINES...

And 3...
2...
1...

Celebrate

For the Dreamers

Back and forth, back and forth
Storms have travelled south and north
I'm not safe from prejudice
My brown skin's their nemesis
Drowning in my family's tears
Neighbors start to disappear
Back and forth, back and forth
Storms have travelled south and north

Doggy paddle, doggy paddle
Whites scream at me to skedaddle
Go back home, but home is here
Home has been The States for years
Wish to work and wish to learn
800,000 float in concern
Doggy paddle, doggy paddle
Whites scream at me to skedaddle

Lightning, thunder, lightning, thunder
I will fight to not sink under
I have dreams and should have rights
I'm an American day and night
We will protest, they will vote
Soy el capitán de este bote
Lightning, thunder, lightning, thunder
I will fight to not sink under

Hurricane Harvey shattered me small
But I got up and mocked the winds
My hopes are a hammer to knock down walls
And dreams are tools to build and mend

A Love Story for Young Men

I'm madly in love with my vulnerability
But it's a forbidden kind of love
Her name is Pain and she pays a visit
Every now and again if I'm fortunate

But I'm betrothed to Pride
And Pride is a jealous and selfish love
And she keeps Pain locked up
And she tells Pain that no man
No *real* man
Will ever want her so long as he has Pride

So Pain waits until nightfall
When Pride is fast asleep
And Pain visits me in my dreams
And begs me to let Pride go
And begs me to accept her beauty
And begs me to embrace her instead

But just when I reach for her with tender heart
Pride jolts up in bed and smacks my wet cheek
And she drags Pain by her hair screaming
Back into captivity to her cage
A cage that's been rusted by alcohol
For many, many years

Pride tells me not to worry
That she will change the locks
That nothing will ever come between us
But it's not the locks I worry about

And while society's eyes watch meticulously over my manhood
I continue to hold Pride the way I should be holding
My sweet, dear, delicate Pain

And someday, I will

For the First Brother

Take my journey and all the lessons I've learned and recorded
And wear them around you like a robe of wisdom
Realize that the bottom of a tequila bottle
Will only tell you which way to go to get to the bottom of a hole

Learn to forgive and trust the water that flows under the bridge
Find something to be passionate about
And chase it like you're a man on fire
You used to love caterpillars and sharks and tornados as a child
Light a match and use that curiosity to make a rope
A rope that you can use to climb up with
Not to hang down from as a noose around your neck

Realize that kindness and generosity are the biceps for a real man
That vulnerability is just extra weight to bench to make you stronger
That friends come and go like the lifespan of a housefly
But families live longer and are full of people to bug you

Because we care
Because I care

We are not so different than you might think we are

For the Second Brother

When you look in the mirror
Remember that the mirror can't speak
There is no mouth but your reflection's
There is only one person in the room
Only one

Remember that confidence doesn't come in a package
And why would it?
Who wants courage that's been contained?
Courage that's been sitting on a dusty shelf
With instructions that tell you to box yourself in?

Don't label yourself the way auctioneers label their cattle
Right before the grand slaughtering
Because when it all ends someday
The labels will mean nothing anyways

Always stand tall on the last laugh
So that when you fall,
And you laugh the hardest, the loudest, and the longest,
You'll make everyone in the room fall into an uncomfortable silence
And you will fall into place on your way to manhood
Gaining the rising respect of others on the journey

There are some days that even I worry
That my weight will crush a scale flat
From the melody that comes with each sad bite I take
But I remember that it is better to bite life with hunger in my eyes
Than it is for life to swallow me whole
And life is too temporary to feed into this

Stand tall, brother, stand tall

For the Third Brother

You are young
But not too young
Not too young to see that the world
Is painted in a kaleidoscope of colors
And that on some days you will see more reds and blues
Than the beautiful golds and violets you'd expect to
But that this is still better than seeing the world in
Black
And
White

We live in a world where "forever" might not be "always"
And where "content soon now" is the new "happily ever after"
But there is still good in this world
And "good" doesn't sound as perfect as "great"
But nothing sweet or beautiful is "great"
And perfection doesn't exist even in fairy tales

When the world gets cold and icy
Have a snowball fight and laugh

When the world starts to boil and burn
Make s'mores and soup, sit and smile

When the world is painfully silent
Sing at the top of your lungs until it hurts

Continue to grow, but not too quickly
Because childhood is the most beautiful part of life
And should be enjoyed in slow motion
Slowly
And
Freely

Candles

After several deep prayers
I head down to the river
And notice the sun has started to yawn
It is now or never
I need to let you go

I place a small box on the shore and whisper to the winds:

Hello, can you hear me?
I know my stories tend to be dramatic
So, I will keep this simple

I'm very grateful for our seventeen years together
Hearing your laughter in the leaves
Feeling your gentle spirit in the breeze
Even the moments you read to me about the little bird
The one who looked for his mother in the faces of strangers

This was a happy chapter in my life

A tear walks down my face slowly
Carrying my heavy heart on its back

The next chapter could be a whole lot happier with you in it
And I don't know if this will help
But I'm sending you my blessings
One for each day I've gone without you

I still need you so that I can say this will be a happy story
One with a happy ending we could all feel
One we can end together

And as Moon rises, I open the box on the shore
And place hundreds of tiny white candles
On pieces of mahogany wood with a poinsettia petal attached
Because both are your favorite

And I light each candle with a steady hand and an empty gaze
And I send them all drifting downstream
With the sounds of owls and crickets and well wishes
So that someday you might hear these echoes
And find your way back

To me

New Angels

When I wanted to keep you off our grass
I should have known whom I was speaking with
I should have known that angels glide over gardens with grace
Instead of stomping on someone's heaven on earth
And spoiling what has survived from Mother Nature's terror

You knew this was sacred ground
And you chose not to build a castle
Until the grass was green again
And the fruit was ripe
And the soil was pure
And the water was fresh and clean

You were delicate with us
Because you were sent by God
To a broken man who was fragile

And you were sweet and you brought light and new seasons
That made the man smile again through a salt-and-pepper beard

You made him feel like a king and you became queen of his heart
And you both ruled over something so special
And he vowed to love you
With a ring as gorgeous as your halo

And God sent others to make a holy choir of laughter
So that our plants would continue to thrive
And everything was beautiful
And peace was once again restored

So I thank the angels and give you my blessings and praise God above
With hallelujahs that light up the land like stars
And I finally believe in miracles again
And second chances

Cup of Tea

I don't remember much about my rebirth
But I know a stork dropped me off on an island at your doorstep
With a note that read: Please assemble, batteries not included

So you and your husband took me in and fixed me up
And you named me Anak and my first word was Ina, followed by Papa
And you fed me Sinigang and cleaned my wounds
While Papa told me tales of his home in the Philippines

And on my first Christmas
You saw that I was shivering
So you crocheted me a scarf and offered me hot tea
And my heart thawed a little

And when I learned how to walk
We had our first dance
And you told me that one day I'd be married
And that we'd dance like this after you give me away
In a beautiful wedding of my own

And I was skeptical
Because family was a foreign language to me for so long
And love was a dialect that I wasn't fluent in just yet

But you believed in me
And you accepted me
And I grew warm and strong
Until I was able to start making you cups of tea
And keeping your spirits warm as a son is supposed to

Because you loved me unconditionally
Because you told me that's just simply
What mothers are supposed to do

I Prayed for Patience and Got You

I.

My island flooded from the rain...
My sanity went down the drain...
I lost my pride and found my pain...

All the voices were calling me nuts...
Tipped over and spilled my guts...
You gave me bandages for all my cuts...

So I fell to my knees and prayed for wisdom
God gave me purpose and gave me a vision
I prayed for courage and God gave me monsters
Gave me a weapon to fight and to conquer
He then gave me family when I prayed for friends
And when I was breaking, they taught me to bend
But just when my doubts and anxiety grew
I prayed for patience and God gave me you...

II.

All the snakes slithered back in the ground...
There's no spiders that hang around...
You made a lost ghost feel like he was found...

All the panic attacks ran away...
All the predators turned into prey...
You could have left me but you chose to stay...

And I fell to my knees and prayed for wisdom
You freed my mind from a terrible prison
I prayed for courage and God gave me monsters
You knew the real me and slayed the imposters
God gave me family when I prayed for friends
You saw me as pure and your love was my cleanse
And just when the cracks and anxiety grew
You put me together with patience and glue...

III.

I'll stay with our ship and drown here with you...
When it comes to marriage, you've changed all my views...
My faith is restored that now one can be two...

So this is to say...
...Thank you

Umbrellas

So it goes...

Dressed in black with white overcoat
I walked through silver haze

I suddenly found myself in a sea of strangers who looked like me
Splashing through murky memories
Swimming together like a school of fish
In the strangest funeral procession
With the coffin up front shielded by a bouquet of umbrellas
Even though the heavy rains had stopped weeks ago

We passed the bench
Where I used to feed breadcrumbs to my sorrows
And we walked into the little white church at the end of the street
A place I've begged for death before
On cold stone floors under jagged pipes

And because I had begged, Death paid a visit
Death took my old broken spirit and
Hung it on a hanger for dry cleaning
And when that wasn't good enough
Death laid me down in a coffin and
Told me to rest for as long as I needed to

And when I finally woke up, I was standing over my corpse
Inside of the little white church
On cold stone floors, under jagged pipes
And I was singing small hymns to both Him and him and whispering:
    Rest in peace to my old shell of a human being
    Pass gently without suffering as the world bleeds orange
    A color that represents possibility
    And new sunrises and new sunsets
    A color more optimistic than filthy blood-red

And when it was over, I stepped outside and took in the fresh air
Today is no longer a day of sour mourning
I came to this funeral to pay sweet respects
To the boy who died so that I could stand strong
In the man I've now become

So it goes...

Into the Eye

After the hurricane left my mind and my surroundings
I don't recall seeing a rainbow
Something I had seen in all the movies
A magical moment of "new promises"

The truth is that the storm left me with
Absolutely
Nothing

And there is nothing beautiful about being left empty
Just ask the singles who were left by their lovers
Or the homeless victims of Harvey
Who can all vouch for what I'm saying

But in the middle of all the chaos
In the quick calm of it all
When Mother Nature tried to catch her breath
In the middle of her tears
Her fits
Her anger
I saw a glimmer of something special

And it wasn't hope
And it wasn't destiny
And it definitely wasn't glory

It was perspective

It was as if I had been
Looking through the wrong end of a telescope for so long
And all I needed to do was turn it around
To see things with crystal clarity
And so I finally did

And in the aftermath, I found reason
I saw empathy from damaged
And power from vulnerability
I saw the pills as an aid
And not as a crutch for being so ill

And most importantly, I saw myself, truly
Without looking in a mirror for someone else

Status Quo II

Someone once asked me what peace feels like
I would imagine it's being of sound mind on a little raft
Paddling softly through wreckage and debris
As cicadas sing and frogs chirp

And I would just lay on my raft
And sip my red wine and nibble saltine crackers
While I take in my surroundings
The way Nature has taken me in

Oh

It's always nice to have a companion with you
Someone to navigate, perhaps
But I'd imagine it wouldn't matter where we'd
Drift off to or
Land or
Just nap in blankets of gentle breezes
Right in the heart of cozy currents

www.ingramcontent.com/pod-product-compliance
Ingram Content Group UK Ltd.
Pitfield, Milton Keynes, MK11 3LW, UK
UKHW020233250726
13967UKWH00001B/337